This is a helicopter, sometimes called a chopper.

Unlike a plane's wings, which are fixed to its sides, a helicopter's wings (called blades) spin around at the top of the helicopter.

spinning blades

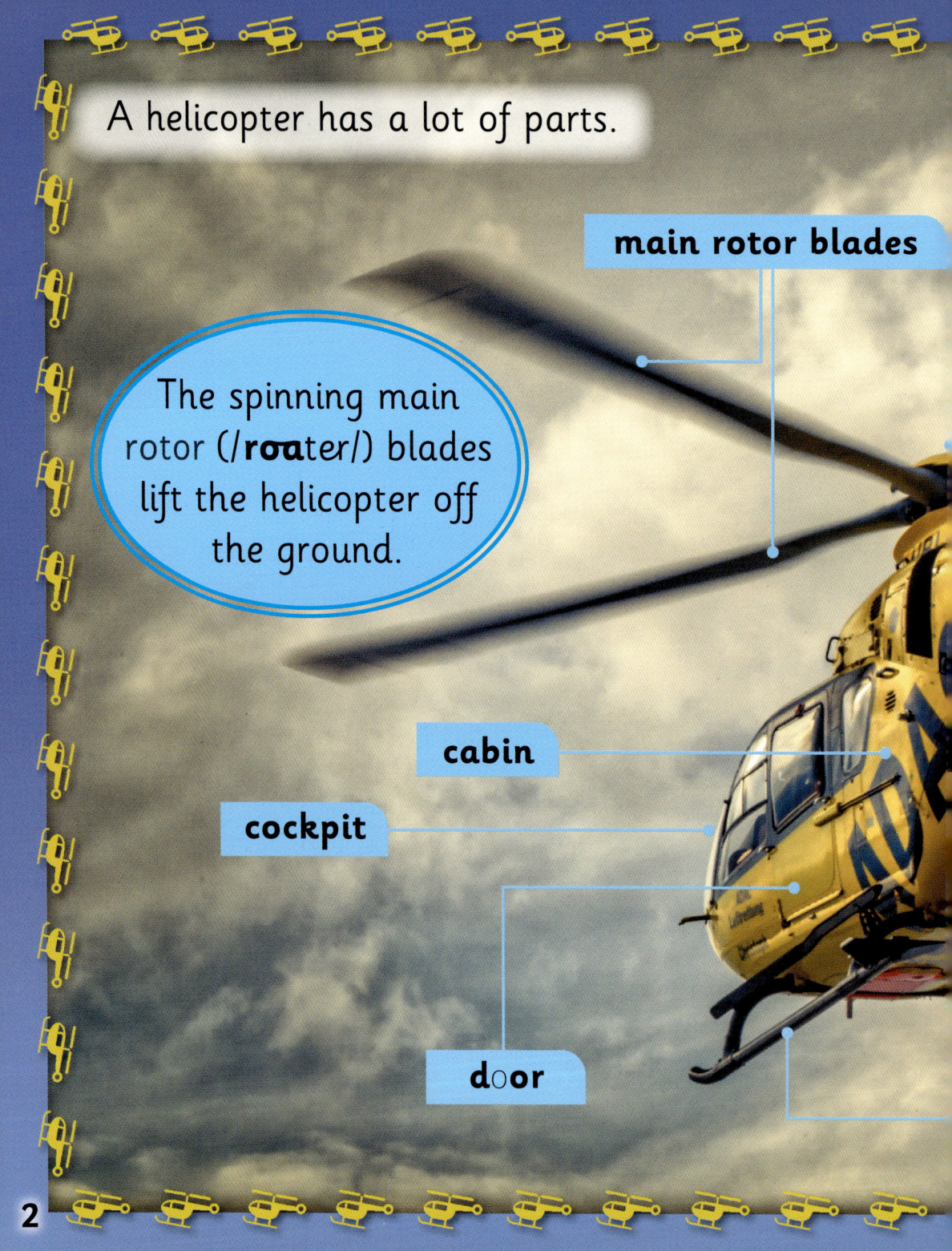

A helicopter has a lot of parts.

main rotor blades

The spinning main rotor (/**roa**ter/) blades lift the helicopter off the ground.

cabin

cockpit

door

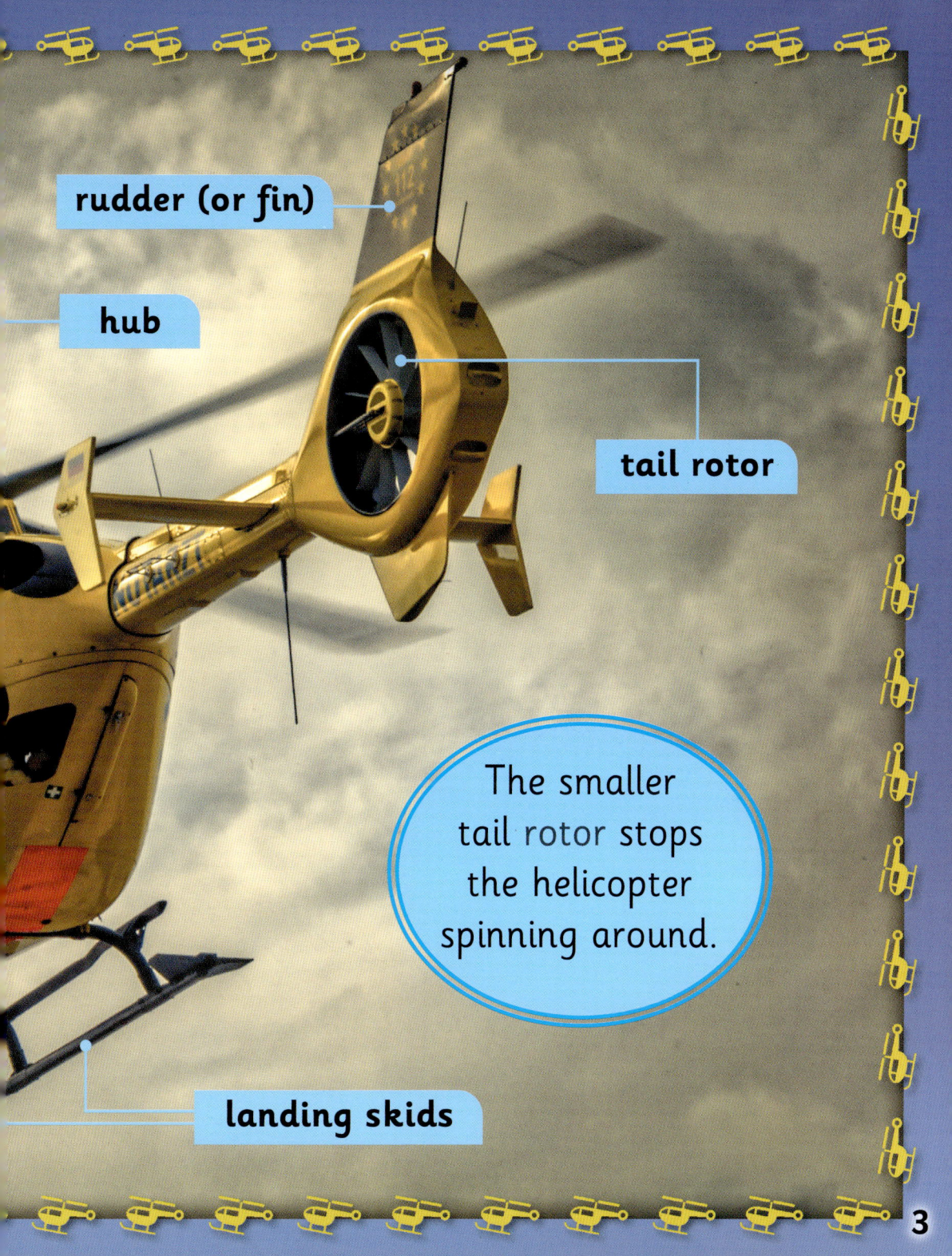

rudder (or fin)

hub

tail rotor

The smaller tail rotor stops the helicopter spinning around.

landing skids

Helicopter cabins are quite small, so they cannot fit in as much as a big plane can.

Look at the size of the person next to the helicopter.

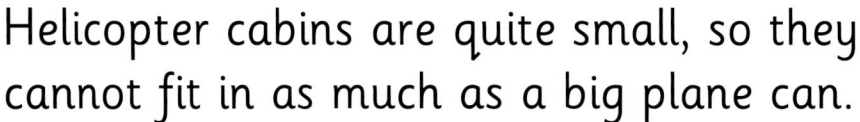

Here is a person next to a plane. You can see that the plane is much bigger than the helicopter.

Helicopters can be very loud, too. The blades at the top shake, and this can make it extremely noisy inside the cabin.

It is important to protect yourself from the loud helicopter noise.

As well as this, helicopters are not as speedy as planes. If a helicopter flies too quickly, it can start to shake.

Despite all of this, helicopters can be very useful.

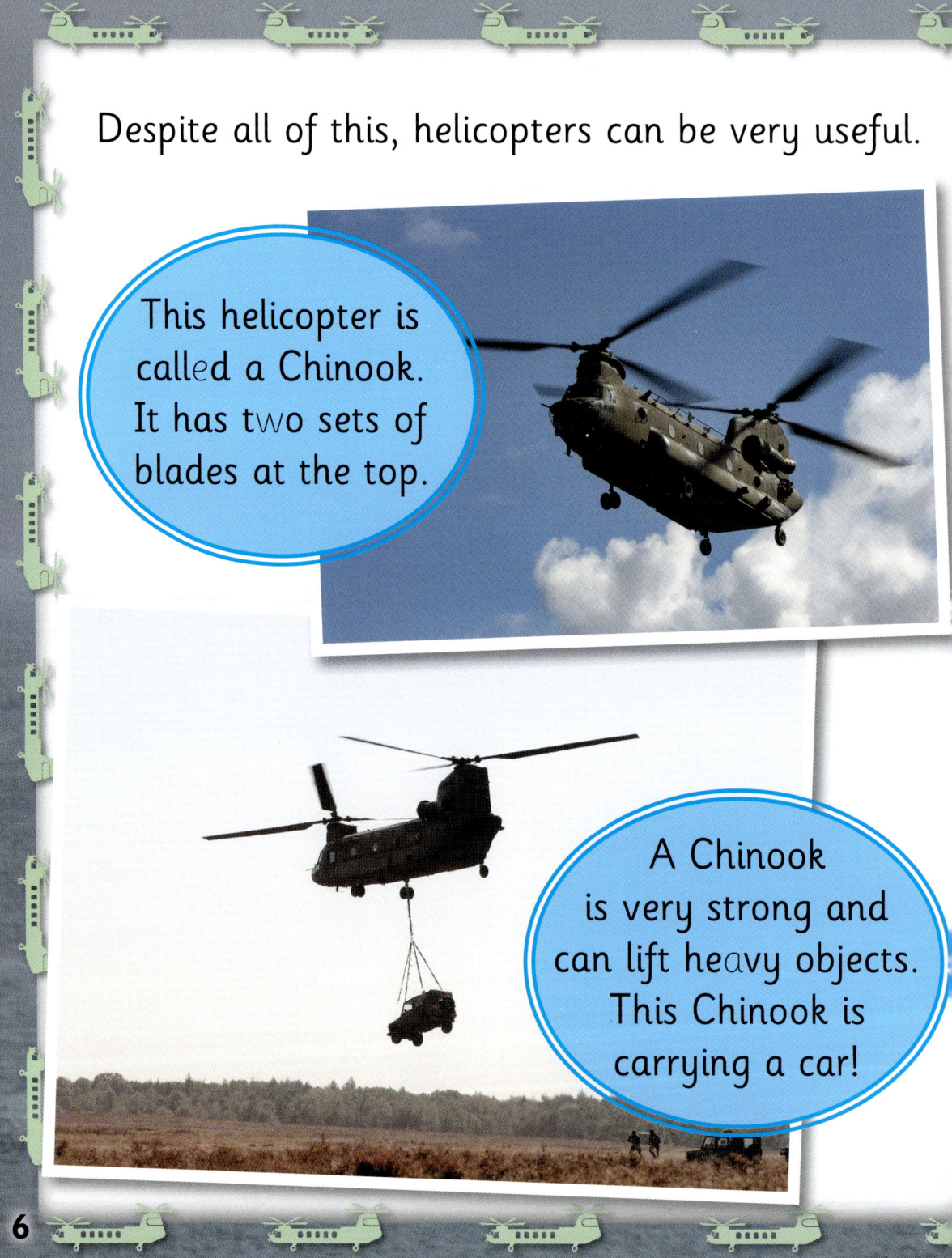

This helicopter is called a Chinook. It has two sets of blades at the top.

A Chinook is very strong and can lift heavy objects. This Chinook is carrying a car!

Helicopters can be used in small, remote spots where planes cannot.

A plane needs to run along the ground before it can take off, but a helicopter can take off and land vertically (straight up or down).

long take off

straight up take off

Helicopters can hover, too. This makes them excellent for search and rescue (looking for someone who is lost or stuck).

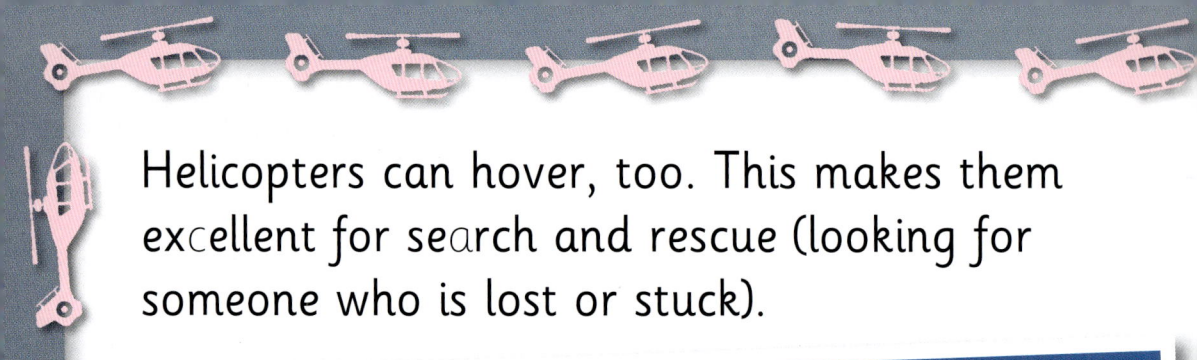

It takes a lot of skill to make a helicopter hover in one spot.

The coastguard can use a helicopter to rescue someone who has fallen off a boat, or is struggling to swim.

coastguard helicopter

Helicopters are used to rescue hikers who are stuck up a mountain, as well.

This is a search and rescue helicopter. There is not a lot of room inside, but everything that is needed is squeezed in.

The pilot (/**pie**lət/) sits here.

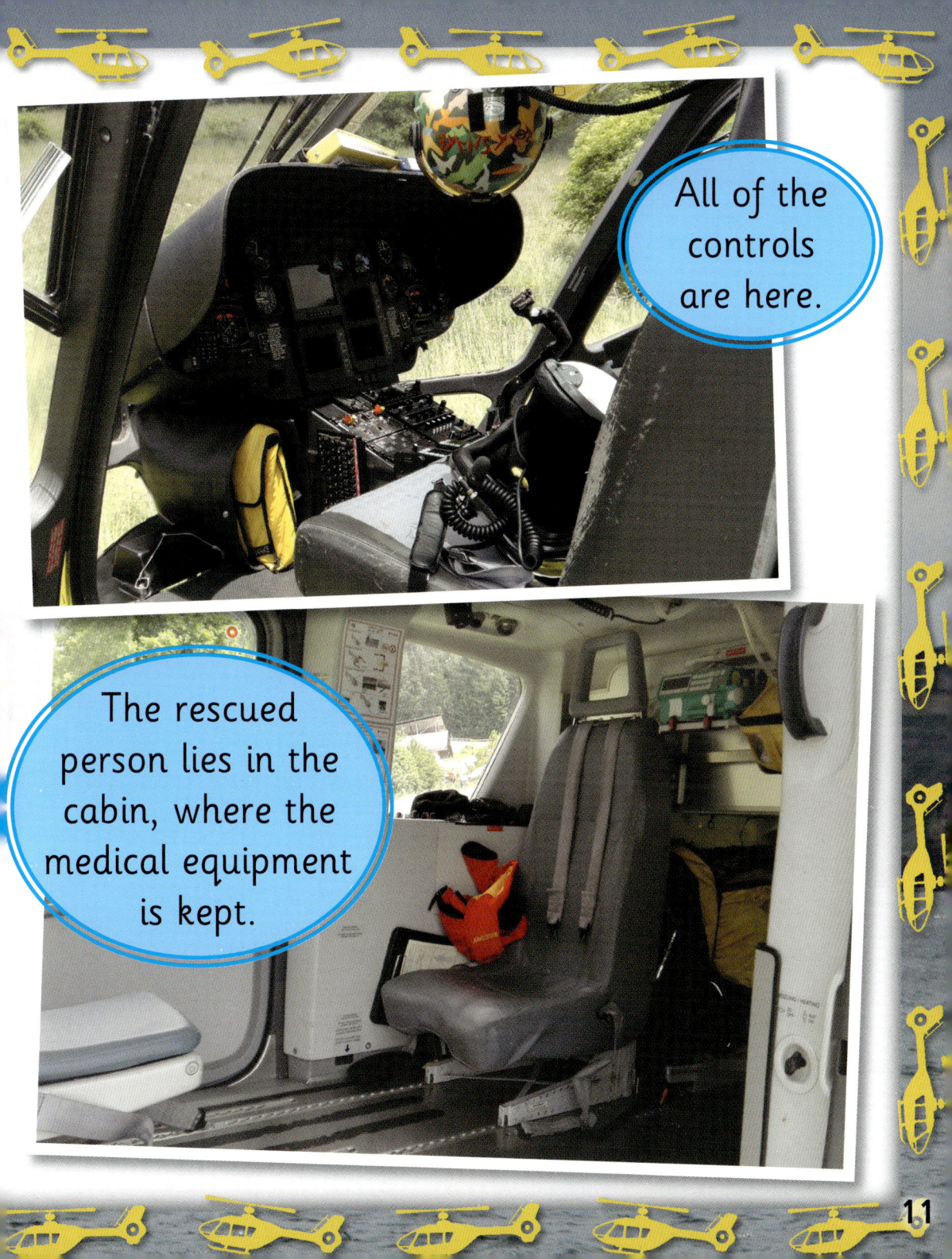

All of the controls are here.

The rescued person lies in the cabin, where the medical equipment is kept.

Sometimes, a helicopter like this is used to get a very ill person to hospital quickly. A paramedic or a doctor flies in the helicopter to help the ill person until they get to the hospital.

stretcher

The stretcher is for the ill person to lie on. The rescuers will carry the person to the helicopter.

This sort of helicopter can be used when there is a forest fire.

thick smoke

flames

A bucket of liquid hangs from the bottom of the helicopter as it flies over the flames.

Often, you can only get on and off an oil rig by helicopter.

Getting to and from an oil rig by boat takes a long time, and it can make you sick. A helicopter trip is much quicker.

helipad

oil rig

Travellers sometimes hire helicopters for short trips.

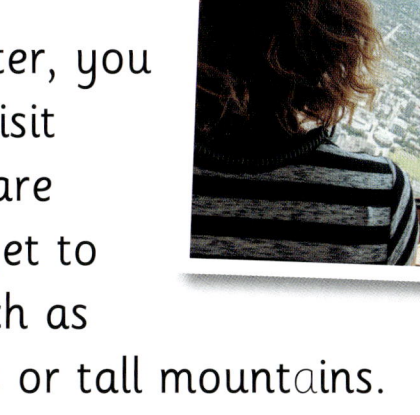

In a helicopter, you can see or visit things that are difficult to get to by road, such as thick jungles or tall mountains.

Helicopter trips are very expensive. You will need to save up for a long time to take a helicopter ride!

So despite being small and noisy, helicopters are a very important form of transport.

In fact, helicopter rescues have saved more than three million (3,000,000) lives around the globe!